My Favorite Wardrobes

By Wilma Brumfield-Lofton

PIAOTT Publishing LLC. Chicago, IL

My Favorite Wardrobes
Wilma Brumfield-Lofton

ISBN: 979-8-9892562-2-8
Copyright © 2024

All rights reserved. No part of this publication may be reproduced or transmitted, or utilized in any form or by any means, electronic or mechanical, including photocopying, recording or by any information storage and retrieval system without permission of the publishers or author.

This Book Belongs To:

_____

THE FRUIT OF THE SPIRIT

"But the fruit of the Spirit is love, joy, peace, forbearance, kindness, goodness, faithfulness, gentleness and self-control. Against such things there is no law." Galatians 5:22-23

THE ARMOR OF GOD

"Finally, be strong in the Lord and in his mighty power. Put on the full armor of God, so that you can take your stand against the devil's schemes. For our struggle is not against flesh and blood, but against the rulers, against the authorities, against the powers of this dark world and against the spiritual forces of evil in the heavenly realms. Therefore put on the full armor of God, so that when the day of evil comes, you may be able to stand your ground, and after you have done everything, to stand. Stand firm then, with the belt of truth buckled around your waist, with the breastplate of righteousness in place, and with your feet fitted with the readiness that comes from the gospel of peace. In addition to all this, take up the shield of faith, with which you can extinguish all the flaming arrows of the evil one. Take the helmet of salvation and the sword of the Spirit, which is the word of God. And pray in the Spirit on all occasions with all kinds of prayers and requests. With this in mind, be alert and always keep on praying for all the Lord's people." Ephesians 6:10-18

My favorite wardrobes are from two collections of designer clothes.

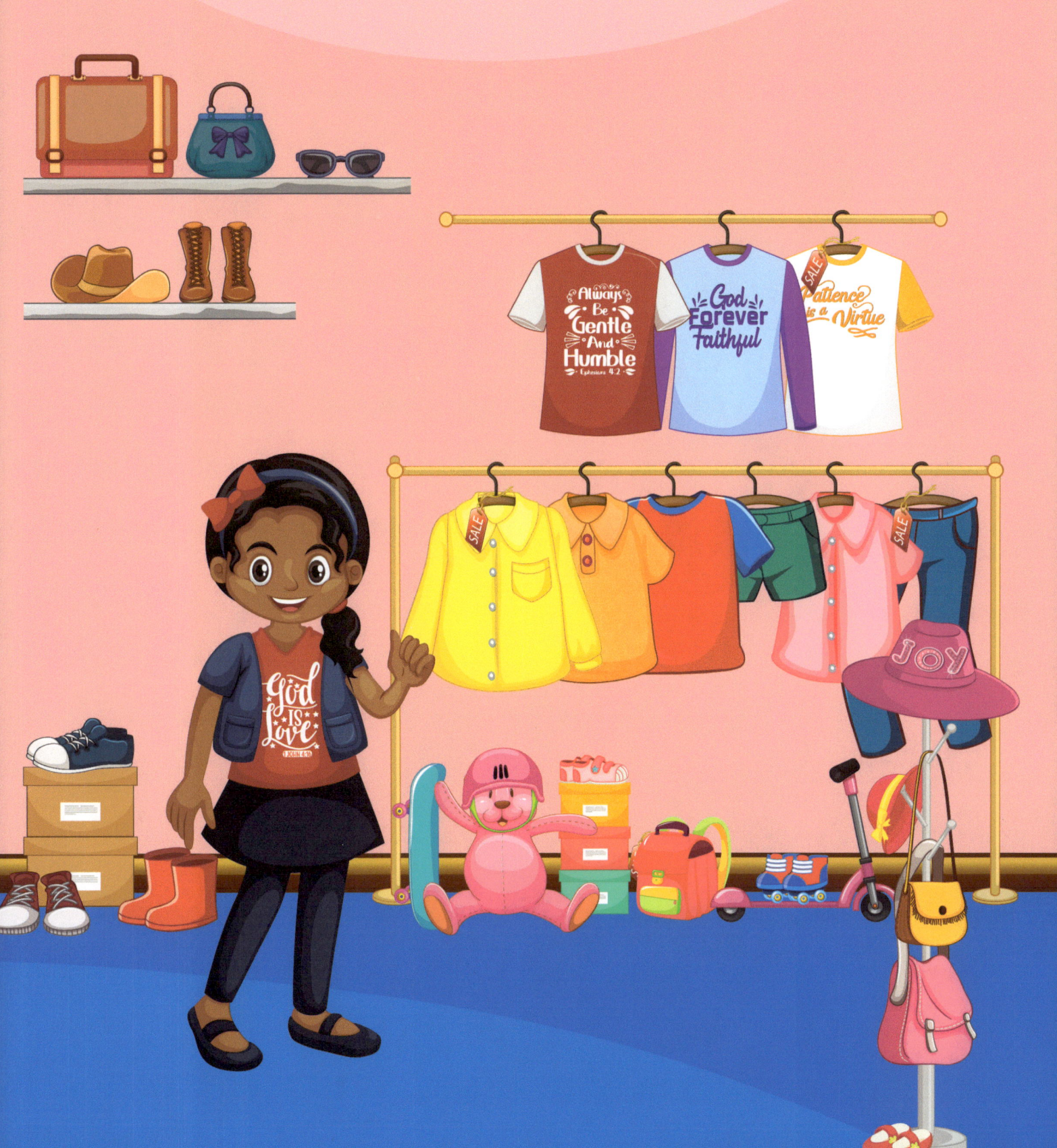

Please come to my fashion show.

Let me and my friends model them for you.

Introducing! The first set of outfits from the Fruit of the Spirit Line. I am wearing "Love," and I will be showering love throughout the room.

Now on the runway, calm and confident is "Peace," walking by Faith.

On the stage now is "Patience" following God's plan and timetable.

Coming with a big smile and a warm and tender heart is "kindness."

Walking the runway with excellence and grace is "Goodness."

Next up is "Faithfulness." A divine quality that means always doing what you say you will do.

Walking eagerly onto the runway is, "Gentleness." Did you know that Jesus himself represents Gentleness. (Matthew 11:29)

Finally we have "Self-Control," the discipline given by the Holy Spirit. (Galatians 5:17)

The next set of clothing is from The Whole Armor Line. I feel very protected wearing my beautiful silver dress made of the Armor of God.

EPHESIANS 6:10-18

Next is London wearing The Breastplate of Righteousness that protects your heart against sin and the enemy's attack.

Next up is Devin wearing The Helmet Of Salvation.

Standing strong with integrity is Lelia wearing The Belt of Truth.

Stepping out on the runway spreading the good news is Reese and he is wearing The Shoes of the Gospel Peace.

Alice is ready for Bible Study with her Sword of The Spirit bookbag.

When you dress in these clothes, from either collections, they will make you feel happy, protected, strong and confident. I wear these clothes everyday!

www.ingramcontent.com/pod-product-compliance
Lightning Source LLC
Chambersburg PA
CBHW041541040426
42446CB00002B/187